W9-BSV-474

Amazing Athletes ✧ Atletas increíbles

Dwyane Wade

Basketball Star ✧ *Estrella del baloncesto*

Mary Ann Hoffman

Traducción al español: Eduardo Alamán

PowerKiDS press™ & **Editorial Buenas Letras**™

New York

Published in 2007 by The Rosen Publishing Group, Inc.
29 East 21st Street, New York, NY 10010

Book Design: Daniel Hosek
Layout Design: Lissette González

Photo Credits: Cover © Doug Pensinger/Getty Images; p. 5 © Jeff Gross/Getty Images; p. 7 © Andy Lyons/Getty Images; p. 9 © Stephen Dunn/Getty Images; p. 11 © Jed Jacobsohn/Getty Images; p. 13 © Eliot J. Schechter/Getty Images; p. 15 © Stuart Hannagan/Getty Images; pp. 17, 19, 21 © Ronald Martinez/Getty Images.

Cataloging Data

Hoffman, Mary Ann, 1947-
  Dwyane Wade : basketball star / Mary Ann Hoffman; traducción al español: Eduardo Alamán — 1st ed.
      p. cm. - (Amazing Athletes / Atletas increíbles)
  Includes index.
  ISBN-13: 978-1-4042-7602-4
  ISBN-10: 1-4042-7602-5
 1. Wade, Dwyane, 1982--Juvenile literature. 2. Basketball players-United States-Biography-Juvenile literature. 3. Spanish-language materials I. Title. II. Series.

Manufactured in the United States of America

Contents

Contenido

Dwyane Wade plays basketball for the Miami Heat. He is an NBA star!

Dwyane Wade juega baloncesto en el Heat de Miami. ¡Dwyane es una estrella de la NBA!

In college, Dwyane led his team to the Final Four. That means his team was one of the best in the country.

En la universidad, Dwyane llevó a su equipo al Final Four. En el Final Four juegan los 4 mejores equipos universitarios del país.

Dwyane was 21 when he joined the Miami Heat in 2003. He was the youngest player ever to start an opening game for the Heat!

Cuando Dwyane llegó al Heat de Miami en 2003, sólo tenía 23 años. Dwyane se convirtió en el jugador más joven en participar en un juego inaugural del equipo de Miami.

9

In 2004, Dwyane was named one of the best rookies in the NBA.

En 2004, Dwyane fue elegido uno de los mejores novatos de la NBA.

Dwyane can jump very high and run very fast. He is sometimes called Flash.

Dwyane puede saltar muy alto y correr muy rápido. Es por esto que a veces le llaman Flash.

13

In 2004, Dwyane was chosen to play for the USA in the Olympics. Team USA came in third.

En 2004, Dwyane fue elegido para jugar en el equipo olímpico de los Estados Unidos. El equipo finalizó en tercer lugar.

15

In 2005 and 2006, Dwyane was named an NBA All-Star.

En 2005 y 2006, Dwyane fue elegido para el Juego de las Estrellas de la NBA.

17

Dwyane scored many points in the All-Star Games.

Dwyane encestó muchas canastas en los partidos del Juego de las Estrellas.

19

Dwyane has won awards for his many skills.

Dwyane ha ganado muchos premios por su habilidad para jugar al baloncesto.

21

Glossary / Glosario

All-Star (AHL–STAHR) One of the best players in a sport.

Final Four (FY-nuhl FOHR) The last four college teams that play to decide which is the best team.

NBA (EN-BEE-AY) The National Basketball Association.

Olympics (uh-LIHM-pihks) A set of games played by sports teams from around the world. The Olympics take place every 4 years.

rookie (RU-kee) Someone who is in their first year in a sport.

---

equipo olímpico (el) El equipo de un país que juega contra otros países durante las olimpíadas. Los juegos olímpicos se llevan a cabo cada 4 años.

Final Four (el) Los cuatro equipos que juegan para decidir cuá será el campeón de baloncesto universitario.

NBA (la) La Asociación Nacional de Baloncesto.

novato, a (el/la) Alguien que participa por primer año en un deporte.

Resources / Recursos

BOOKS IN ENGLISH / LIBROS EN INGLÉS

Savage, Jeff. *Dwyane Wade*. Minneapolis, MN: First Avenue Editions, 2006.

Smallwood, John. *Before They Were Stars*. New York: Scholastic, Inc., 2003.

BOOKS IN SPANISH / LIBROS EN ESPAÑOL

Suen, Anastasia. *La historia del baloncesto*. Rosen Publishing/Editorial Buenas Letras, 2004.

Index

Índice

SOUTHSIDE BRANCH LIBRARY
PHONE: (205) 933-7776